OSHUN

IFÁ AND THE SPIRIT OF THE RIVER

AWO FÁ'LOKUN FATUNMBI
OMO AWO FATUNMISE, ILE IFE,
BABALAWO ÈGBÈ IFÁ, ODE REMO,
OLÚWO ILÉ ÒRÚNMÌLÁ OSHUN, OAKLAND, CA

OSHUN
IFA AND THE SPIRIT OF THE RIVER

Awo Falokun Fatunmbi

Original Publications
P.O. Box 134
Jericho, NY 11753
www.Occult1.com
www.OriginalPublicationsw.com

The spells, charms and ingredients herein are true to tradition in metaphysics. They are offered as curio and for their legendary value. No supernatural claims are made.

ISBN: 0-942272-32-3

ACKNOWLEDGEMENTS

The material in this book is primarily based on oral instruction from the elders of *Ifá* in Ode Remo, Ogun State, Nigeria and Ile Ife, Oshun State, Nigeria. In appreciation for their time, patience and loving concern for my training and spiritual guidance I say: *A dúpé Ègbè Ifá Ode Remo, Babalawo* Adesanya Awoyade, *Babalawo* Babalola Akinsanya, *Babalawo* Saibu Lamiyo, *Babalawo* Odujosi Awoyade, *Babalawo* Olu Taylor, *Babalawo* Abokede Arabadan, *Babalawo* Biodun Debona, *Babalawo* Oluwasina Kuti, *Babalawo* Afolabi Kuti, *Babalawo* Fagbemi Fasina, *Babalawo* Oropotoniyan and all the members of *Egbe Apetebi Ode Remo.*

Additional material in this book is based on instruction from the elders of Ile Ife, Oshun State, Nigeria. In appreciation to them I say: *A dúpé Awon Ifá Fatunmise Ègbè Ifá Ilé Ife, Jolofinpe* Falaju Fatunmise, *Babalawo* Ganiyu Olaifa Fatunmise, *Babalawo* Awoleke Awofisan Lokore, *Babalawo* Ifaioye Fatunmise, *Babalawo* Ifanimowu Fatunmise, *Babalawo* Ifasure Fatunmise, *Babalawo* Adebolu Fatunmise and all the members of *Egbe Apetebi Awon* Fatunmise.

A special thank you to the members of *Ilé Òrúnmìlà Oshun* for their continuing support and understanding: *Olori Yeye Aworo* Timi Lade, *Apetebi Orunmila, Iya l'Orisha* Oshun Miwa (Luisah Teish), *Eko'fa Iya l'Orisha* Omijinka, *Iya l'Orisha* Iya Oshun Iya Oshogbo, *Iya l'Orisha* Shango Wenwa, *Awo* Ifa Ijalagun Molu, Leona Jacobs-White, Nzinga Denny, Earthea Nance, Vance Williams, Blackberri, Salim Abdul-Jelani, Rebecca Schiros, Carol Lanigan, Zena Attig, Thisha, Rose Schadt, Xochipala Maes Valdez, Dee Orr, Nina Heft, Isoke and Earl White. A grateful thanks to *Awo* Medahochi and *Iya* Omolade.

A final thank you to Maureen Pattarelli for her work in editing this manuscript. *Orunmila a buru, a boye, a bosise.*

Awo Fá'lokun Fatunmbi
Oakland, CA

TABLE OF CONTENTS

INTRODUCTION

Oshun is the Spirit of the river in the West African religious tradition called "*Ifá*". The word *Oshun* is the name given to describe a complex convergence of Spiritual Forces that are key elements in the *Ifá* concept of fertility and the erotic. Those Spiritual Forces that form thē foundation of *Oshun's* in the Spirit Realm relate to the Creation of new forms through the interaction between polar opposites. According to *Ifá*, Creation occurs through the polarity between the Forces of expansion and contraction. Together these Forces create light and darkness, which in turn sustains and defines all that is. *Ifá* scripture often refers to Forces of expansion as "*Orisha Okunrin*", which means "Male Spirit" and to Forces of contraction as "*Orisha Obinrin*", which means "Female Spirit". Both forms of Spiritual Power are considered of equal importance in the evolution of all that exists. One is not better than the other because it is only through the balance of opposites that life comes into Being.

There is no literal translation for the word *Ifá*. It refers to a religious tradition, an understanding of ethics, a process of spiritual transformation and a set of scriptures that are the basis for a complex system of divination.

Ifá is found throughout the African diaspora where it spread as an integral part of Yoruba culture. The Yoruba Nation is located in the Southwestern region of Nigeria. Prior to colonization, the Yoruba Nation was a federation of city-states that was originally centered in the city of *Ilẹ̀ Ifẹ*. According to *Ifá* myth, the Yorubas migrated to *Ilẹ̀ Ifẹ* from the east under the leadership of a warrior chief named *Oduduwa*. It is difficult to date the time of the Yoruba move into West Africa because of limited archaeological research on the subject. Estimates range from between sixteen hundred to twenty-five hundred years ago. It is likely that migration took place over a number of generations. As the population grew, each new city-state that became a part of the Yoruba federation was governed by a chief called "*Oba*". The position of *Oba* is a form of hereditary monarchy and each *Oba* goes through an initiation that makes them a spiritual descendant of *Oduduwa*.

Traditional Yoruba political institutions are very much integrated with traditional Yoruba religious institutions. Both structures survived British rule in Nigeria, and continue to function alongside the current civil government.

Within the discipline of *Ifá*, there is a body of wisdom called "*awo*", which attempts to preserve the rituals that create direct communication with Forces in Nature. *Awo* is a Yoruba word that is usually translated to mean "secret". Unfortunately, there is no real English equivalent to the word *awo*, because the word carries strong cultural and esoteric associations. In traditional Yoruba culture, *awo* refers to the hidden principles that explain the Mystery of Creation and Evolution. *Awo* is the esoteric understanding of the invisible forces that sustain dynamics and form within Nature. The essence of these invisible forces are not considered secret because they are devious, they are secret because they remain elusive, awesome in their power to transform and not readily apparent. As such they can only be grasped through direct interaction and participation. Anything which can be known by the intellect alone ceases to be *awo*.

The primal inspiration for *awo* is the communication between transcendent Spiritual Forces and human consciousness. This communication is believed to be facilitated by the Spirit of *Eşu* who is the Divine Messenger. Working in close association with *Eşu* is *Ogun* who, is the Spirit of Iron. *Ogun* has the power to clear away those obstacles that stand in the way of spiritual growth. According to *Ifá*, the work done by *Ogun* is guided by *Ochosi*, who as the Spirit of the Tracker has the ability to locate the shortest path to our spiritual goals. The essential goal that *Ochosi* is called upon to guide us towards is the task of building "*ìwa-pẹ̀lẹ́*", which means "good character". This guidance takes the form of a spiritual quest which is called "*ìwakiri*". One of the functions of *Obatala* is to preserve the Mystic Vision that to those who make the quest of *ìwakiri* in search of *ìwa-pẹ̀lẹ́*.

The power of *Oshun* is described by *Ifá* as one of many Spiritual Forces in Nature which are called "*Orisha*". The word *Orisha* means "Select Head". In a cultural context, *Orisha* is a reference to the various Forces in Nature that guide consciousness. According to *Ifá*, everything in Nature has some form of consciousness called "*Orí*". The *Orí* of all animals, plants and humans is believed to be guided by a specific Force in Nature (*Orisha*), which defines the quality of a particular form of consciousness. There are a large number of *Orisha* and each *Orisha* has its own *awo*.

The unique function of *Oshun* within the *Orisha Awo* (Mysteries of Nature) is to provide the spark of passion that attracts the Forces of expansion and contraction to each other. This attraction occurs on all levels of existence from the polarities which guide the formation of planets to the attraction between men and women. *Oshun* as the source of passion is the Goddess of the Erotic, and according to *Ifá* the power of the erotic motivates the *Orisha* in every realm of Being.

Ifá teaches that all Forces in Nature come into Being through the manifestation of energy patterns called *Odu*. *Ifá* has identified and labeled 256 different *Odu* which can be thought of as different expressions of consciousness. But because consciousness itself is generated by *Obatala* (The Chief of White Cloth), every *Odu* contains an element of *Obatala's aşę* (power). In metaphysical terms, this means that all of Creation is linked to *Obatala* as the Source of Being. *Ifá* teaches that all forms of consciousness contain a spark of *aşę* (spiritual power) from *Obatala*, and it is this spark that links everything that is to its shared Beginning.

According to *Ifá* each *Orisha* is linked to *Obatala* in a way that defines the function of the *Orisha*. The relationship between *Obatala* and *Oshun* places the realm of the erotic in the context of good character. This does not mean that *Ifá* has either a repressive or pejorative view towards sexuality. It does mean that the development of good character is a factor in the exploration and expression of erotic impulses.

I.

ALỌ IRINTÀN OSHUN
FOLKTALES OF THE SPIRIT OF THE RIVER

A. *OSHUN IJO ILẸ́* — The Spirit of River Dances in the Village of Women

All the Immortals gathered in *Ọ̀run* on the day that they were engaged in a battle with the Village of Women. It was a battle that the Immortals knew that they could never win. *Oba Ọ̀run* (the Chief Heaven) asked the *Orisha* to make the journey from *Ikolẹ Ọ̀run* (the Realm of the Ancestors) to *Ikolẹ Aye* (Earth) in an effort to end the war.

Shango (the Spirit of Lightning), *Ògún* (the Spirit of Iron), *Omolu* (the Spirit of Infectious Disease) and the *Ibora Egun* (the Spirit of all those Warrior Ancestors who have passed) agreed to join hands in the battle against the Village of Women. They fought with courage and conviction but met with bitter defeat.

Yemoja (the Mother of Fish), *Oya* (the Spirit of the Wind) and the *Iyami* (the Spiritual Mothers of all those ancestors who have passed) agreed to join hands in the battle against the Village of Women. They fought with courage and conviction but met with bitter defeat.

When all of the *Orisha* and *Egun* from *Ikolẹ Ọ̀run* (the Realm of the Ancestors) returned from their battle with the Village of Women, they refused to engage in further combat. At that point, it was *Oshun* who said that she would put an end to the battle with the Village of Women. *Oshun* placed a calabash of water on her head and danced from *Ikolẹ Ọ̀run* (the Realm of the Ancestors) to *Ikolẹ Aye* (Earth). As she approached the village of women, she continued to dance and sing, using the calabash as a drum. When she had reached the center of the village, the women joined with *Oshun*. They danced and sang to the sound of her drum. The women of the village followed *Oshun* to *Oshun's* shrine where they sing and dance for her to this day.

Commentary: Some stories about *Oshun* that are popular in the West tend to characterize her as "superficial" and "self-centered". In this story, *Oshun* is presented as a powerful warrior who is able to resolve a conflict that has defeated all the Spiritual Forces of Heaven. According to *Ifá*, each of the *Orisha* has a warrior aspect that is used to protect the *Orisha* from extinction. This story makes it clear that not all forms of protection involve warfare, or what is traditionally identified as "aggressive" behavior.

This story also involves two aspects of female power that recur throughout *Ifá* literature. It is not common in Western myth to find stories about a group of women who have the collective strength to defeat all the Forces of Heaven. In traditional Yoruba culture, women's secret societies are centered around Mysteries involving menstrual blood. This tradition has been disrespected by Western writers who tend to dismiss these societies as forms of "witchcraft".

In reality, the female secret societies are an integral part of traditional Yoruba religious and political life. It is the women who place the *adẹ* (crown) on the *Oba* (senior village chief). The women are given this role because the *adẹ* contains the *aṣẹ* (spiritual power) of protection that only comes through female power. When this power is invoked as a means of protection, it is extremely effective and extremely volatile. The ritual means of harnessing this power once it has been unleashed is part of the *awo*, or Mystery of *Oshun*. That is why initiates of *Oshun* generally have high ranking positions within the female secret societies.

This story is a metaphorical presentation of an aspect of Female power that remains taboo to the uninitiated.

B. *OSHUN SEKẸSẸ* — The River Goddess is the Owner of Mystery

It was *Obatala* (The Chief of White Cloth) who learned the

awo merindinlogun (the mystery of cowrie shell divination) from the *Orisha* (The Immortals) who lived in *Ikolẹ Ọ̀run* (the Realm of the Ancestors). On the day that *Obatala* came to live in *Ikolẹ Aye* (earth), it was he alone who knew *awo Odu* (the mystery of sacred scripture), *awo etutu* (the mystery of making offerings to the ancestors), *awo ebo* (the mystery of making offerings to *Orisha*), and *awo Igbodu* (the mystery of initiation).

The people of *Ikolẹ Aye* (Earth) would turn to *Obatala* whenever they needed the guidance of *merindinlogun* (divination). But it was *Obatala's* habit to wander the streets, the forest, and travel from town to town. Often the people of *Ikolẹ Aye* would come to the home of *Obatala* in search of guidance from *merindinlogun* (divination) and discover that he was not at home.

It was *Oshun* (The Goddess of the River) who followed *Obatala*on the day that the people of the earth wanted *merindinlogun* (divination) to become available to all *Omo Orisha* (devotees of the Immortals). *Oshun* (The Goddess of the River) followed *Obatala* to the river where he took off his white robes and entered the water. As *Obatala* swam, *Oshun* asked *Eṣu* (The Divine Messenger) to convince *Obatala* that he should teach her the *awo merindinlogun* (the mystery of divination).

Eṣu told *Oshun* to return to her home and take a bath in *oyin* (honey). Then *Eṣu* walked through the brush and picked up *Obatala's* clothes. He took the clothes to the home of *Oshun* and placed them on *Ojubo Orisha* (her sacred shrine). When *Obatala* came out of the river he saw that his clothes were missing and followed *Eṣu's* footprints to the home of *Oshun*.

Obatala knocked on *Oshun's* door and demanded his clothes. *Oshun* answered the door dripping in *oyin* (honey) from her bath. It was on that day that *Obatala* agreed to teach *Oshun* the *awo merindinlogun* (the mystery of divination).

To this day those who worship *Oshun* say, "*Iba Oshun Olodi, Oshun sekẹsẹ*", which means, "Praise to the Goddess of the River, Owner of Fresh Water and Guardian of Mystery".

Commentary: In Nature the river is the source of fresh water, and fresh water is the foundation for the fertility that creates life on land. It is water that nourishes the vegetation that produces the oxygen, which allows for the precipitation that maintains the ecological balance that sustains life on Earth. It is water that nourishes the embryo in the womb. *Oshun* is the personification of this fertility as it exists throughout Nature. The river in all of its manifestations brings life together in a state of mutual balance and interdependency. It is this interaction that forms the basis for the *Ifá* concept of "*ifẹ*", which means "love".

Oshun as the incarnation of both fertility and love represents the impulse to maintain balance and harmony within the natural environment. When this impulse is translated into a communal environment it represents the motivating factor for social justice. In the Myth of *Oshun* the mystery of divination is limited to *Obatala*. By using her allure and charm, *Oshun* makes divination available to all the Immortals. The result is communal access to the power that comes from knowledge of the inner secrets of Nature. Whenever this power becomes limited to a particular segment of society, the balance and harmony that is ordained by Natural Law becomes disrupted.

In traditional Yoruba political structure it is the priestesses of *Oshun* who have a key role in maintaining the communal standards of justice and equality.

II.

ÌMỌ̀ OSHUN
THE THEOLOGICAL FUNCTION OF THE SPIRIT OF THE RIVER

A. *OSHUN 'YÀNMỌ́-ÌPIN* — The Spirit of the River and the Concept of Destiny

The *Ifá* concept of "*àyànmọ́-ìpin*", which means "Destiny," is based on the belief that each person chooses their individual destiny before being born into the world. These choices materialize as those components that form human potential. Within the scope of each person's potential there exists parameters of choice that can enhance or inhibit the fullest expression of individual destiny. *Ifá* calls these possibilities "*ọna ipin*", which means "road of destiny". Each decision that is made in the course of one lifetime can effect the range of possibilities that exists in the future, by either limiting or expanding the options for growth.

It is within the context of choice, or what is known in Western philosophical tradition as "free will" that *Ifá* recognizes a collection of Spiritual Forces called "*Ibora*". In Yoruba, the word *Ibora* means "Warrior". Traditionally the *Ibora* include *Eşu, Ògún* and *Ochosi*. *Eşu* is the cornerstone that links the *Ibora* as they relate to the issue of spiritual growth. According to *Ifá*, each moment of existence includes a wide range of possible actions, reactions and interpretations. Those moments which require decisive action are described in *Ifá* scripture as "*ọna'pade*", which means "junction in the road". Whenever a person who is trying to build character through the use of *Ifá* spiritual discipline reaches *ọna'pade*, it is customary to consult *Eşu* regarding the question of which path will bring blessings from *Orisha*.

Ifá teaches that blessings come to those who make choices that are consistent with their highest destiny. Within Yoruba culture it is understood that an individual's highest destiny is based on those choices that build "*ìwa-pẹ̀lẹ́*", which means "good character". Those who develop good character are often described as weaving white cloth, which means creating purity and spiritual elevation in the world. The collective impact of those who weave white cloth is entering into a state of mystical union with the Chief, or the Source of White Cloth who is called *Obatala*. This is true for everyone, even those who worship other *Orisha*. *Ifá* scripture clearly suggests what all of the *Orisha* exist as an extension of the power of consciousness that is created by the *aşẹ* (power) of *Obatala*.

It is the function of *Oshun* to generate the passion that makes the development of good character an attractive task. *Ifá* teaches that everyone who comes to *Ikolẹ Aye* is entitled to a good life. *Ifá* scripture defines a good life as the blessings of abundance, long life and children. *Oshun* has the task of generating the passion that leads to the creation of children, and She also has the task of generating the creative passion that defines abundance as a way of life. It is *Oshun* who inspires the artist, it is *Oshun* who creates the attraction to fine clothes and jewelry, and it is *Oshun* who encourages communities to join together in celebration of the changes in the seasons. Some religious traditions try to suppress these fundamental human needs, but in *Ifá* they are praised in the name of *Oshun*.

B. *OSHUN 'ẀAKIRI* — The Spirit of the River as the Source of the Erotic

Ifá cosmology is based on the belief that the Primal Source of Creation is a form of Spiritual Essence called "*ąsẹ*". There is no literal translation for *aşẹ*, although it is used in prayer to mean "May it be so".

Ifá teaches that the visible universe is generated by two dynamic forces. One is the force of "*inàlo*", which means "expansion", and the other is the force of "*isoki*", which means "contraction". The first initial manifestation of these forces is through "*ìmo*", which means "light", and through "*aimoyé*", which means "darkness". In *Ifá* myth, expansion and light are frequently identified with Male Spirits called "*Orisha'ko*". Contraction and darkness are frequently identified with Female Spirits called "*Orisha'bo*". Neither manifestation of *aṣẹ* is considered superior to the other and both are viewed as essential elements in the overall balance of Nature.

In *Ifá* cosmology both *ìmo* and *aimoyé* arise from the matrix of the invisible universe which is called "*Imolẹ*", which means "House of Light". Within the house of light there is an invisible substance that transforms spiritual potential into physical reality. The invisible substance that moves between these two dimensions is called *aṣẹ*, and it is *Obatala* who brings the *aṣẹ* of Light into the world.

In his role as Creator of the substance of the Universe, *Obatala* is called "*Oloono Ọ̀run*", which means "Owner of that which emerges from the Invisible Realm". Science teaches that energy in the Universe creates radiation and that radiation forms a spectrum of vibrations called light waves. The visible spectrum of light is only a small fragment of the light spectrum. This suggests that the majority of Forces that exist in Creation are invisible to the human eye. Some of these Forces guide the structure of atoms, and some of these Forces guide the structure of galaxies. To call *Obatala* "*Oloono Ọ̀run*" is to say that *Obatala* is the Source of all those visible and invisible Forces that generate the physical universe.

Science tells us that atoms unite to form elements. *Ifá* teaches that the poser of attraction that leads to the desire of atoms to form elements is the erotic impulse called *Oshun*. Science tells us that the gases dispersed by the sun formed the planets. *Ifá* teaches that the power of attraction that caused these gases to unite in the shape of a sphere is the erotic impulse called *Oshun*. Science tells us that single cell life forms evolved into fish, birds and the animals that walk the earth. *Ifá* teaches that the power of attraction that leads life forms to reproduce is the erotic impulse called *Oshun*.

Without the inspiration of *Awo Oshun* (Mystery of the Spirit of the River), there would be no diversity in Creation.

C. *AWO IYAMI* — The Mystery of Woman's Power

1. *AWON IYAMI* — The Social Function of Women's Mysteries

In traditional Yoruba culture the preservation of Female Mysteries is generally referred to as "*Awo Iyami*", which translates literally to mean "Mystery of My Mothers". Most anthropological references to *Iyami* translate the term to mean "witch". This is generally done in a negative pejorative context which reflects the bias of the anthropologist more than it reflects the true meaning of this important *Ifá* concept.

Ifá scripture says that all *Orisha* come to the world through the mothers. This means that every deified ancestor, regardless of their gender is born of a woman. It is the care and nurturing that comes from the mothers that places each child firmly on the path of developing good character. This is an important social function that is honored through the traditional structure of *Ifá* religion. Most of the religious institutions that honor Female Power did not survive in the West and this has given some Western *Ifá* and *Orisha* worshipers the mistaken impression that *Ifá* is a patriarchal tradition based on the concept of male superiority. This impression is totally inaccurate with regard to the understanding and practice of *Ifá* and *Orisha* worship in Africa.

Ifá cosmology is based on the concept of balance between forces of expansion and contraction. Forces of expansion are generally associated with Male Spirits and Forces of contraction are generally associated with Female Spirits. All ritual work done within *Ifá* and *Orisha* spiritual discipline is a reflection of the interaction between forces of expansion and contraction as they exist in Nature.

This has been a very difficult concept for most anthropologists to grasp because most *Ifá* and *Orisha* ceremonies which are performed in public represent a small portion of the ritual process. For example, when *Egungun* masquerades through the streets of a particular city, the ancestral mediums, the mediums escorts and the drummers that perform for the mediums are men. The masquerades occur during the day and can continue for several days at a time. It is during the night hours when the mediums are secluded from public observation that the priestesses involved in *Egungun* ritual participate as part of the invocation process.

During the initiation into *Ifá*, which appears to outsiders as an all male fraternity, women have key roles in the ritual process. Discussion of their function is taboo, but it can be said that they have a key role in the protection of the initiate during that part of the ritual when the initiate is most vulnerable to negative spiritual influences.

Most, but not all traditional political leaders are male. The High Chiefs are called *Oba*, and they must go through an initiation process that spiritually transforms them into a direct descendant of *Oduduwa*, who is considered the original Father of Yoruba culture. Again, it is taboo to give details, but female initiates play a key role in the initiation of the *Oba*. In addition, the *Oba* cannot sit in his official capacity of Chief without wearing an *Adẹ* (crown). It is the women initiates who piace the *Adẹ* on the *Oba's* head. This task has both a political and spiritual function. Politically it creates a balance of power because the women can decline to crown the Chief until areas of dispute are settled. Spiritually it ensures that the balance of Forces that exist in Nature remain reflected in the political process.

Oshun initiates have a key role in *Awo Iyami* because it is *Oshun* who has the *aṣẹ* (spiritual power) to take prayers directly to *Olu* (The Source of Creation).

2. *ÌMỌ̀ AWON IYAMI* — The Theological Function of Women's Mysteries

Ifá teaches that human life is part of the cycle of *atunwa* (reincarnation). Those spirits who return to *Ikolẹ Aye* (Earth) from *Ikolẹ Ọ̀run* (The Invisible Realm of the Ancestors) always pass through the gateway of the mother's womb. From a Western scientific point of view the womb is the incubator for the interaction between egg and sperm. *Ifá* teaches that the physical interaction between egg and sperm triggers a spiritual opening that allows the *emi* (spirit) of an individual ancestor to animate the embryo.

In very literal terms this suggests that the womb is a direct physical link between *Ikolẹ Aye* (Earth) and *Ikolẹ Ọ̀run* (The Invisible Realm of the Ancestors). This link is established each time a woman experiences menstruation. If there is no pregnancy when this gateway is opened the power of this connection may be used to invoke abundance and to ensure that issues of respect and justice towards women are maintained. *Ifá* considers this gateway to be the most primal source of *aşe* (spiritual power) available for use in ritual process. The ways in which this is done is taboo to the uninitiated. Those who would denigrate this aspect of *Ifá* are expressing their own lack of understanding.

III.

Ọ̀NA OSHUN
THE ROADS OF THE SPIRIT OF THE RIVER

In the scripture of *Ifá* the folklore and sacred history of the *Orisha* often describes them in different manifestations. These manifestations are called "*Ọ̀na Orisha*", which means "Roads of the Forces of Nature". For example, the River as a Force in Nature may be flowing, filled with water and pouring topsoil along the shoreline. The River may be low, empty while it waits for rain. They are both manifestations of the Spirit of the River in different seasons of its yearly cycle. The sacred shrine at *Osogbo* sits on the *Oshun* River at the place where *Ifá* says that *Oshun* first came to Earth. At *Osogbo* the *Iya l'Orisha* (Priestesses) say that *Oshun* has forty-one roads and each of these roads is remembered with a separate shrine built along the *Oshun* River.

Among the more common roads of *Oshun* are the following aspects of the Spirit of the River:

1. *Oshun Yẹyẹ Moro* — The Spirit of the River, Mother of the Mirror.
2. *Oshun Kayodẹ* — The Spirit of the River, Owner of the Dance.
3. *Oshun Migwa* — The Spirit of the River guides my Character.
4. *Oshun Ibu* — The Spirit of the River who Lives Where the River Meets the Sea.
5. *Oshun Funmikẹ* — The Spirit of the River who Blesses us with Children.
6. *Oshun Olodẹ* — The Spirit of the River who Lives in the Depths of Water (Mermaid).

7. *Oshun Edẹ* — The Spirit of the River who Creates Beauty and Elegance.
8. *Oshun Funkẹ* — The Spirit of the River who Teaches the Mystery of the Erotic.
9. *Oshun Ibu Kolẹ* — The Spirit of the River who Transforms.

IV.

ILẸ́ ORISHA
THE SHRINE OF THE SPIRIT OF THE RIVER

A. *ILẸ́ ORISHA ADURA* — Shrine for Prayer and Meditation to the Spirit of the River

Those who are interested in honoring *Oshun* who have no access to either *Ifá* or *Orisha* elders can set up a shrine that may be used for meditation and prayer. The shrine can be used as a focal point for meditation that can lead to a deeper awareness, appreciation and understanding of *Oshun's* role and function within Nature. Such a shrine should be set up in a clean place and make use of either white, yellow or green cloth (separately or in combination) as a setting for other symbolic altar pieces.

Oshun is associated with the River, so anything that has been discovered in or near fresh water may be placed on the shrine. *Oshun* also makes use of mirrors and fans as extensions of Her dance and aspects of Her *Awo* (Mystery).

Oshun is also associated with birds, especially the vulture, the peacock, the quail and the humming bird.

The shrine should be a place where it is possible to find inspiration for what *Ifá* calls "*orí opa*", which means "creative abundance". This term is a reference to the state of inspiration that comes to those who have a deep appreciation for the mystery of the erotic.

B. *ILẸ́ ORISHA ORIKI* — Shrine for Invocation to the Spirit of the River

Shrines which are used for the invocation of *Oshun* are

constructed from consecrated religious elements that are presented to a devotee during initiation. These objects may vary, but they generally include a pot that contains the sacred power objects that attract the *aşẹ* (spiritual essence) of *Oshun*; a brass bell, a yellow horse tail fan, a feather fan (usually peacock), and brass jewelry.

The *Ifá* calendar is based on a five day week and those who have received the *aşẹ* of *Orisha* generally greet their shrine each morning and say invocations to their shrine every five days. The invocations are called "*Oriki*", which means "praising the consciousness". An example of *Oriki Oshun* is as follows:

ORIKI OSHUN

Ìbà Oshun awura Olu.
I respect the Spirit of the River, the central inspiration of Creation.
Oloriya Igun,
Chief Priestess of the Vulture,
Erẹwa Obinrin.
Source of Women's power.
Awẹdẹ ko to wẹ'mo.
Your sacred herb is my inspiration.
Yẹyẹ mi, a dupẹ.
I thank my Mother.
Aşẹ.
May it be so.

C. *ADIMU OSHUN* — Offerings to the Spirit of the River

In all forms of *Ifá* and *Orisha* worship it is traditional to make an offering whenever guidance or assistance is requested from Spiritual Forces. *Adimu* is a term that is generally used to refer to food and drink that is presented to the Spirit of a particular shrine. The idea behind the process of making an offering is that would be unfair to ask for something for nothing. Those who have an unconsecrated shrine to *Oshun* can make the offering in their own words. Those who have a consecrated shrine to *Oshun* may use the

Oriki for *Oshun* when making a presentation of *Adimu*. This is usually done when a prayer requesting assistance from *Oshun* is made. The answer to the prayer can then come through divination.

The following offerings may be used as *adimu Oshun*:

1. Honey
2. Pumpkin
3. Melon
4. Champagne
5. River water

D. *EBO OSHUN* — Life Force Offerings to the Spirit of the River

There is a wide range of ritual procedure in Africa involving the worship of *Orisha*. Many of the differences in ceremonial process reflect regional differences in emphasis rather than essence. The term, "life force offering", is used in reference to the fact that many *Orisha* rituals requires a preparation of a feast or communal meal. Whenever this occurs the blood from the animal that is used for the meal is given to *Orisha* as an offering. This offering is considered a reaffirmation between *Ikole Ọ̀run* (The Realm of the Ancestors) and *Okole Aye* (Earth). This covenant is an agreement between Spirit and humans that Spirit will provide food for the nourishment of people on earth. In return the worshipers of *Ifá* and *Orisha* agree to respect the spirit of the animal who provided the food and agree to elevate the spirit of that animal so it will return to provide food for future generations.

Whenever a life force offering is made to any of the *Orisha*, an invocation is generally made to *Ògún* as part of the process. This is a grossly misunderstood aspect of *Ifá* and *Orisha* worship which has suffered from negative stereotypes in the press and the media. It is part of *awo Ogun* (Mystery of the Spirit of Iron) to learn the inner secrets of making life force offerings. When an *Orisha* initiate is making a life force offering it should include an invocation for the *Odu Ogunda*. If the initiate is using the *Lucumí* system of *Merindinlogun*, the invocation would be to *Ogunda*

Meji. In *Ifá* the invocation for life force offerings is to *Ogunda-Irẹtẹ*.

The life force offerings used for *Oshun* are as follows:

1. Hen
2. Goat

E. *ÌWẸ OSHUN* — Cleansing for the Spirit of the River

Ifá and *Orisha* makes extensive use of a wide range of cleansing rituals that are designed to clear away the negative effects of illness, sorrow, grief, anger and contamination by negative spiritual influences. The most fundamental form of cleansings takes the form of blessing water. This means that the water is charged with the power of prayer to accomplish a specific purpose. Once the water has been blessed it can be used to wash specific parts of the body such as the head, the hands or the feet, or it can be used for bathing. Cleansings for *Oshun* would use river water which has small amounts of honey added to it.

Those who are uninitiated may say a prayer to *Oshun* in their own language and breathe the prayer into the water. The healing effect of the water can be enhanced by adding either coconut milk, snail juice or powdered milk.

Those who are initiated may add their *aşẹ* to the water with the following prayer:

Ìbà şẹ Oshun, mo juba.
I praise the Spirit of the River and give respect.
Ìbà şẹ omi tutu, mo juba.
I praise the cool water and give respect.
Mo ni (your name.)
I am (your name.)
Omi tutu, mo be yin,
Cool water, I beg you,
Fun mi ni alafia.
Bring me peace.

Fun mi ni ilera.
Bring me a stable home.
Fun mi ni ori 're.
Bring me the blessings of wisdom.
Fun mi ni ori tutu.
Bring me the blessing of calmness.
Oshun ba m'ka omi l'akaaki.
Spirit of the River make the water medicinal.
Lagbo ofẹ alagbo wo 'ya wo omo.
Goddess who freely gives medicine to cure mother and child.
Ba mi dẹ 'di agbo omo mi k'o mu, k'o ki.
Bless my child's medicine and make it strong.
Mo ti de ìwa-pẹ̀lẹ́.
I am a person of good character.
Oshun a ji ala, mo dupe.
I thank the Spirit of the River for bringing the blessing of health.
Aṣẹ.
So be it.

V.

ORISHA 'GUN

THE SPIRIT OF THE RIVER AND THE MEANING OF SPIRIT POSSESSION

Those who practice the religion of *Ifá* in Africa are generally members of a society that worships a single *Orisha*. These societies are usually referred to by the term "*ẹ̀gbẹ̀*", which means "heart", as in the expression "the heart of the matter". Those who worship *Oshun* would be members of *Ẹ̀gbẹ̀ Oshun*. There are regional differences in the use of this term. In some areas societies of *Oshun* worship might be called either "*Ilẹ́ Oshun*", meaning "House of *Oshun*", or "*Awon Oshun*", meaning "Those who worship *Oshun*".

Regardless of the name used, each of these societies preserves the oral history, myth and wisdom associated with *Awo Oshun* (The Mystery of the River). Part of the wisdom that is preserved concerns the discipline used to access altered states of consciousness. Western literature on *Orisha* tends to refer to these states as "possession". This term is inadequate to describe the various forms of trance that are used to assist the *Orisha* worshiper in their understanding of the Mysteries of Being.

Ifá teaches that it is possible to access both *Orisha* (Forces in Nature) and *Egun* (ancestors) through the disciplined use of dreams. The word "*ala*" is used in Yoruba to mean "dream". *Ala* is the last part of the word *Obatala* and it suggests that the dream state is closely associated with the source of consciousness itself. The word "*alala*" is the word for "dreamer". Because dreamer has a positive connotation in *Ifá*, the word *alala* is a reference to those who are able to make effective use of dreams. *Alala* appears to be a contraction of *ala* and *ala*. In Yoruba words are often repeated for emphasis or to establish relative relationships. To use the word *ala* twice suggests that the reference to dreamer is an expression of the belief that dreams can access the true source of inner thoughts.

Ifá teaches that it is possible to develop an ongoing relationship with *Orisha* that makes a person sensitive to the influence of *Orisha* on a daily basis that effects their immediate environment. In English this is usually referred to as a highly developed intuition. The Yoruba word for intuition is "*ogbon inu*", which translates literally to mean "the stomach of the earth". *Ifá* metaphysics is based on the idea that those Forces in Nature that sustain life on earth establish certain guidelines for living in harmony with Creation. The development of a sensitivity to these forces is part of the discipline of *Orisha* worship, and this sensitivity is called "*ogbon inu*".

There are a number of words that are used to describe those altered states that are commonly referred to as possession. In conjunction with *Orisha*, the word "*jogun*", meaning either, "I possess", or "I have", is used to describe a close spiritual connection with Spirit. The phrase "*Orisha'gun*", is used to describe those who have assumed the characteristics of a particular *Orisha*.

The more common term for possession is "*ìní*". This word reveals the *Ifá* perspective on those trance states represent a deep connection with the *aşẹ* (power) of *Orisha*. The word *ini* appears to be a contraction of "*i*", which is a personal pronoun, and "*ni*", which is the verb "to be". To use the phrase "I am" as a reference to possession suggests that what is frequently thought of as an intrusion from outside forces is more accurately understood as a process of unlocking the *awo* (mystery) of the inner self. *Ifá* teaches that every person comes to Earth with a spark of divinity at the foundation of their *orí* (inner spirit). Part of the discipline of *Orisha* worship is to access this spark of divinity. This is generally accomplished through initiation, which is designed to guide the initiate towards access to the inner self, which in turn forms a transcendent link to that *Orisha* which is closest to the consciousness of the initiate.

Those who have been through initiation for *Oshun* can enhance their access to *ini* at the same time that offerings are made to their shrine on a five day cycle. This is done by saying *Oriki Oshun* in front of the initiates *Oshun* shrine. When the *Oriki* is spoken a candle is lit near the *Orisha* pot and a glass of water is placed near the candle. After the *Oriki* has been completed, the initiate breathes into the glass of water and says the word "*to*", which means "enough". The word *to* is used at the end of *Oriki* as a seal or lock to attach the invocation to whatever it is spoken on to.

Using the index finger, the ring finger and the little finger on the left hand, the initiate dips the fingers in the water and runs the water from between the forehead across the top of the head and down the back of the neck. When the fingers are between the eyebrows say, "*iwaju*", which is the name of the power center at the forehead. When the fingers are on the top of the head say, "*ori*", which is the name of the power center at the crown of the skull. When the fingers are on the back of the neck say, "*ipako*", which is the name of the power center at the base of the skull.

A sample of the type of *Oriki* that is used for this process is as follows:

Ìbà Oshun Sekęsę,
I respect the Spirit of the River, Goddess of mystery,
Latojoku awędę wę 'mo.
Who cleans me from the inside out.
Eni idę ki su omi a san ręrę.
She who makes brass uses water to bring good fortune.
Oshun o pę o.
Spirit of the River I am calling you.
Oshun o pę o.
Spirit of the River I am calling you.
Oshun o pę o.
Spirit of the River I am calling you.
Oshun o pęlę o.
Spirit of the River I am greeting you.
Oshun ro.
Spirit of the River descend.

Mbe mbe ma yẹyẹ, a dupẹ.
Eternal Mother I give thanks.

Aṣẹ.
May it be so.

Oshun — The Spirit of the River

VI.

ORIN OSHUN
SONG FOR THE SPIRIT OF THE RIVER

1. Call: ***Aladę yę aladę yę moro.***
(Chief Mother, Chief Mother speak.)
Response: Repeat.
Call: ***Aladę yę iyami olu yęyę***
(Chief Mother, my Mother, Elder of Mother.)
Response: ***Aladę yę aladę ye moro.***
(Chief Mother, Chief Mother speak.)
Call: ***Alade koyu iyami moro.***
(Chief Mother, my Mother speak.)
Response: ***Alade ye alade ye moro.***
(Chief Mother, Chief Mother speak.)
Call: ***Yęye yęyęo aremi iyami aşę komaya.***
(Mother, Mother, my Friend, my Mother bring the power of the Mothers.)
Response: ***Yęyę yęyęo aremi yeye komaya.***
(Mother, Mother, my Friend, my Mother bring the power of the Mothers.)

2. Call: ***Oshun sherekętę me owo Oshun sherekętę me owo omidara odara ogue Oshun sherekętę me owo omidara odara ogue.***
(Spirit of the River bring me abundance, Spirit of the River bring me abundance, water of transformation good things come from the Spirit of the River, bring me abundance and the water of transformation.)
Response: Repeat

Oshun with Vulture and Peacock

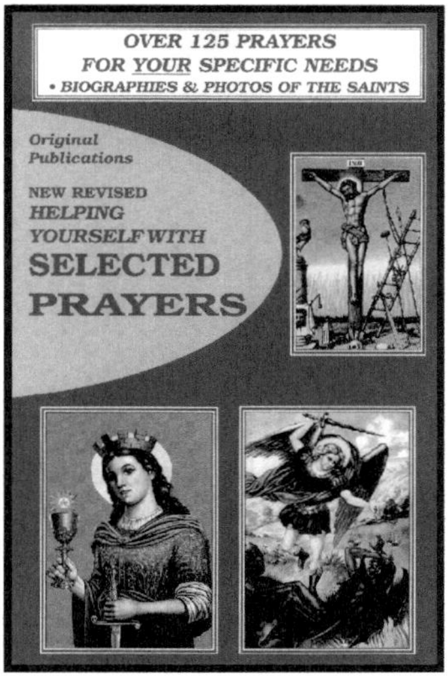

ITEM #214
$12.95

HELPING YOURSELF WITH SELECTED PRAYERS

Now over 130,000 in print!

The New Revised Helping Yourself with Selected Prayers provides an English translation for over 125 prayers of various religious beliefs. These prayers will provide a foundation upon which you can build your faith and beliefs. It is through this faith that your prayers will be fulfilled.

An index is provided to help the reader find the appropriate prayer for his or her particular request. The index also includes suggestions regarding the appropriate candle to burn while saying a particular prayer.

The devotions within these pages will help you pray consciously, vigorously, sincerely and honestly. True prayer can only come from within yourself.

ISBN 0-942272-01-3 5½"x 8½" 112 pages $12.95

ITEM #224
$9.95

Revised and Expanded

Success and Power Through Psalms

By Donna Rose

For thousands of years, men and women have found in the Psalms the perfect prayer book, possessing wisdom applicable to every human situation. Wise men and women of deep mystical insight have also learned to decipher the magical formulas David and the other Psalmists hid behind the written words. These formulas help the seeker solve everyday problems, achieve higher states of consciousness, gain material and spiritual wealth, as well as help defend himself or herself against psychic attacks and all manner of dangers.

The Revised and Expanded edition of Donna Rose's classic offers over 300 simple to perform magical rituals to help you manifest all of your desires using the magical powers of the psalms.

ISBN 0-942272-79-X 5½"x 8½ $9.95